D1713543

Fun with Chemistry

Testing and Checking

Amanda Vink

COMPUTER KIDS
Powered by Computational Thinking

PowerKiDS
press.

Published in 2018 by The Rosen Publishing Group, Inc.
29 East 21st Street, New York, NY 10010

Book Design: Jennifer Ryder-Talbot
Editor: Caitie McAneney

Photo Credits: Cover, p. 10 jarabee123/Shutterstock.com; p. 5 Syda Productions/
Shutterstock.com; p. 9 Samuel Borges Photography/Shutterstock.com; p. 13, 15 ©
iStockphoto.com/fstop123; p. 16 © iStockphoto.com/jayjayoo_com; p. 18-19, 20 ©
iStockphoto.com/jarabee123.

                    Library of Congress Cataloging-in-Publication Data

Names: Vink, Amanda.
Title: Fun with chemistry: testing and checking / Amanda Vink.
Description: New York : Rosen Classroom, 2018. | Series: Computer Kids: Powered by
Computational Thinking | Includes glossary and index.
Identifiers: LCCN ISBN 9781538353059 (pbk.) | ISBN 9781538323991 (library bound) |
ISBN 9781538355619 (6pack) | ISBN 9781508137290 (ebook)
Subjects: LCSH: Chemistry--Juvenile literature. | Chemistry--Experiments--Juvenile
literature.
Classification: LCC QD35.V56 2018 | DDC 540--dc23

Manufactured in the United States of America

CPSIA Compliance Information: Batch #WS18RC: For Further Information contact Rosen Publishing, New York, New York at 1-800-237-9932

Table of Contents

You Can Be a Chemist!

Chemistry is a science that deals with the **composition**, structure, and properties of substances, and **chemical reactions** that occur between them. Chemistry is all around us! You can even study chemistry in your own body. For example, the human body is made up of about 60 percent water. Water is a **compound** of two elements, which are **materials** that can't be broken down further. The elements in water are hydrogen and oxygen.

Chemists are scientists that often test chemical reactions. They have to be **persistent** when they're working on an experiment. They also have to be very **observant**, especially when they are looking for changes in matter. You can be a chemist if you have these qualities!

4

Chemistry is all around us!
Most things you experience with your
five senses involve chemical reactions.

The Scientific Method

Scientists use the scientific method to test a hypothesis, or an educated guess about why something happens. The scientific method is important because it outlines the same **procedure** that all scientists should follow for **accurate** results.

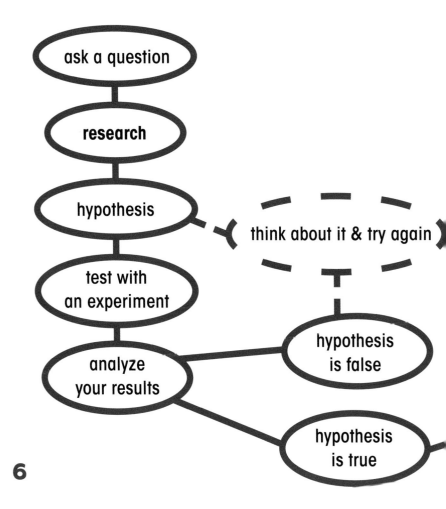

The scientific method we use today was created over a long time, with ideas from many scientists. Scientists often work together to develop better ways to solve a problem. Using the scientific method helps chemists remember exactly what they did in an experiment so they can repeat it. They may also repeat someone else's experiment. Repetition, or doing something over and over, is very important in science. It's the only way to show that something is always true.

This flowchart of the scientific method helps you picture the steps.

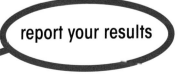

report your results

The Slime Experiment

Slime is a mix of glue and water with borax. Borax is another name for a type of **mineral** called sodium borate. When mixed together, the hydrogen in the ingredients links up, which is why slime sticks together.

You can use the scientific method to make slime! Your goal is to change the thickness of the ingredients. Slime should stay together, but it should also ooze in a changeable state. It should be sticky, but not so sticky that it sticks to your hands. The first step in the scientific method is coming up with a question that should be answered by the experiment. Your question will be: What happens when you mix borax, glue, and water?

Your question will determine your hypothesis.
Make sure to think about your question first!

This slime is a polymer made from glue and borax.

What Are Polymers?

The next step in the scientific method is to research. Let's learn important facts about slime. What is slime, anyway?

Slime is a polymer. "Poly" means "many," and "mer" means "part." A polymer has many parts! It is made up of small molecules, or the smallest pieces making up a chemical, which hook together in a long chain. Polymer molecules can either hook together in one long, straight chain or they can hook into a blob. Polymers can be made of many different kinds of molecules. Depending on what makes up a polymer, it could look and feel very different. Plastic is a polymer. Rubber is a polymer. Your DNA is a polymer, too!

Let's Make Slime!

Now that you have researched your question, you can come up with a hypothesis. Think about the information you learned about polymers. Using this information, you might **hypothesize** that by mixing borax, water, and glue, the molecules will link together and you will end up with slime. Your hypothesis is important. If the experiment doesn't result in slime, you'll want to know what went wrong.

Get ready to test your hypothesis! During this process, you'll need to observe what happens with the addition of each ingredient. Make sure to take notes!

First, fill a small cup with water and add a spoonful of borax powder. Does anything happen? The borax powder **dissolves** in the water!

Make sure an adult helps you when you work with chemicals.

A Chemical Reaction

In another bowl, add about 1/4 cup of water to 1 ounce of Elmer's glue. What happens to the glue when water is added? Mix it with a spoon. Does it look any different?

If you'd like, you can add food coloring to the glue solution. A solution is the liquid that you get from dissolving something in water or another kind of liquid. Add one tablespoon of the borax solution you created earlier. As you start to mix the two together, make note of what happens. Your slime should form as the hydrogen molecules start linking together. It might become so thick that you have to stop using your spoon and start mixing with your hands!

> **Slime should thicken as you mix the ingredients together.**

Check Your Slime!

Did your slime experiment work? You'll need to check the results using your observational skills. Look at your slime carefully and take note of its texture, or feel. Record some of its qualities. Is it more wet or dry? Does it stick to itself or to your hands?

If the experiment worked, congratulations! You made slime and proved the hypothesis to be true. If the experiment didn't result in slime, don't worry! This is an opportunity to put your chemistry skills to the test. What do you think went wrong? Was there too much or not enough of an ingredient? What could you try differently? This is a case in which you need to be persistent!

Sometimes you need to make changes while testing your experiment.

Test Your Slime!

You can continue collecting data for your research. Test your slime to see what it can do. How far can you pull it apart before it breaks? Really put it to the test. Does it break apart quickly or slowly? Does it stick to various surfaces in different ways? How long does it take for **gravity** to flatten it like a pancake? As you play with the slime, does it change over time?

Take note of your findings so you can look back on them. These kinds of notes help scientists compare their findings. It's time to look at all the data and come to a conclusion. Your conclusion for this experiment should be: "When you mix borax, water, and glue, it makes slime."

How does your slime behave?

Another Kind of Slime

Scientific experiments should be repeatable. You'll have to be persistent and do the experiment multiple times. Does it work the same every time or are there differences? You can also play with the ingredients to see what happens. You can make different kinds of slime! Let your curiosity guide you in testing many different mixtures.

You can change the color of slime by using different food coloring. By adding glitter, you can make "galaxy slime" that looks like stars. You can make "fluffy slime" by adding shaving cream to the mixture!

Real chemists have to present their findings. After you finish your experiments, share your results with your class, your friends, and your family.

> **You can make different kinds of slime by slightly changing the ingredients.**

Chemistry in the World

Now that you know how to use the scientific method, you can apply it to other experiments and processes in your life. Look around you. Do you wonder how something works? Do you want to test a chemical reaction? You'll have to be persistent and observant to test the world around you.

You can replicate, or repeat, the experiments of other scientists. You can also come up with a new hypothesis and test it by doing an experiment. As you play with new ideas and share your results, you may even be adding to the field of science. Can you imagine your ideas helping other new chemists think of their own experiments? Chemistry is a fun way to test matter!

Glossary

accurate: Free from mistakes.

chemical reaction: When chemicals have an effect on one another.

composition: The makeup of a chemical compound.

compound: Something formed when more than one element or part comes together.

dissolve: To mix with a liquid so that the result is a liquid that is the same throughout.

gravity: The force that pulls objects toward the ground on Earth.

hypothesize: To make an educated guess about the outcome of something.

material: Something from which something else can be made.

mineral: A solid chemical element or compound that occurs naturally.

observant: Paying close attention to something.

persistent: Continuing to do something despite challenges.

procedure: A set of steps followed in an exact order.

research: Studying to find something new.

Index